Daddy, Daddy, Can You Touch the Sky?

Daddy, Daddy, Can You Touch the Sky?

Written and Illustrated by
Jonathan Kellerman
and Jesse Kellerman

BANTAM BOOKS
NEW YORK · TORONTO · LONDON · SYDNEY · AUCKLAND

Daddy, Daddy, Can You Touch the Sky?
A Bantam Book / August 1994

BOOK DESIGN BY ANTLER & BALDWIN DESIGN GROUP.

Library of Congress Cataloging-in-Publication Data

Kellerman, Jonathan
   Daddy, daddy, can you touch the sky? / written and illustrated by
Jonathan Kellerman and Jesse Kellerman.
   p. cm.
   Summary: Six poems designed to develop strong identity
concepts.
   ISBN 0-553-07324-9
   1. Identity (Psychology)--Juvenile poetry. 2. Children's poetry,
American. [1. American poetry.] I. Kellerman, Jesse. II. Title.
PS3561.E3865D33 1994
811'.54--dc20   94-9556
                                                      CIP
                                                      AC

Published simultaneously in the United States and Canada

Bantam Books are published by Bantam Books, a division of Bantam
Doubleday Dell Publishing Group, Inc. Its trademark, consisting of the
words "Bantam Books" and the portrayal of a rooster, is Registered in
U.S. Patent and Trademark Office and in other countries. Marca
Registrada. Bantam Books. 1540 Broadway, New York, New York 10036.

PRINTED IN THE UNITED STATES OF AMERICA

FFG   0 9 8 7 6 5 4 3 2 1

Thank you, Faye,
for being such a fabulous friend, wife, and mother.

Thank you, Jesse,
for teaching me how to snare an ectoplasm
with verve and panache.

Thank you, Rachel,
for your gracious and wise artistic counsel.

Thank you, Ilana,
for giving me the idea for this book and
for serving as my always-patient technical consultant.

Thank you, Aliza,
for not eating the rocks in my nineteenth-century
porcelain hibachi.

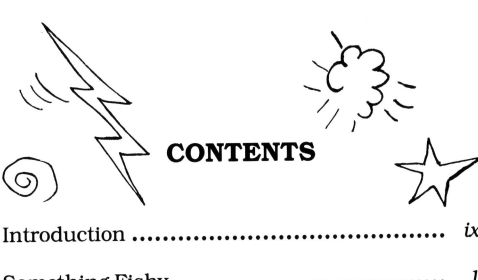

CONTENTS

INTRODUCTION

One of a child's most important "jobs" is to develop a sense of identity—a stable and comforting notion of who he or she is in relation to loved ones, friends, and the surrounding world.

During my years as a clinical child psychologist and as a father of four wonderful kids, I've learned firsthand how essential a robust identity is in promoting optimal self-esteem, a strong conscience, good decision-making skills, and the ability to cope with stress.

Though the "who-am-I" quest continues throughout adulthood, a great deal of personality is formed during the first six or seven years of life, and it is during this period that the *foundation* of identity is firmly set in place. Accordingly, *Daddy, Daddy, Can You Touch the Sky?* was written with the preschooler and younger primary-school child in mind.

The verses and illustrations in this book grew out of discussions with children and have been designed to stimulate children's thoughts, fantasies, and comments about identity concepts: sameness and difference, reality and imagination, the limits of parental power, the wondrous nature of unconditional parental love, how to contend with—and *master*—things that go bump in the night. Equally important, they are meant to be great fun.

Share the verses with your child and use them as jumping-off points for all kinds of discussions—from serious to downright silly. Encourage your child to offer his or her own questions, answers, additions, deletions, drawings, wisecracks, doggerel, free verse, story lines, punch lines.

Most of all, enjoy!

Sincerely,

Jonathan Kellerman

Something Fishy

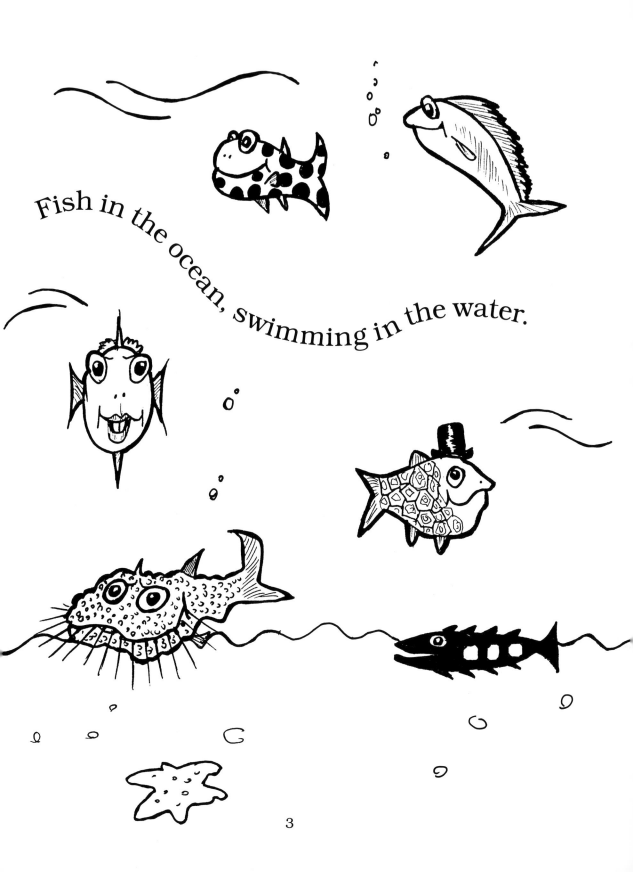

Fish in the ocean, swimming in the water.

Some are sons,

some are daughters.

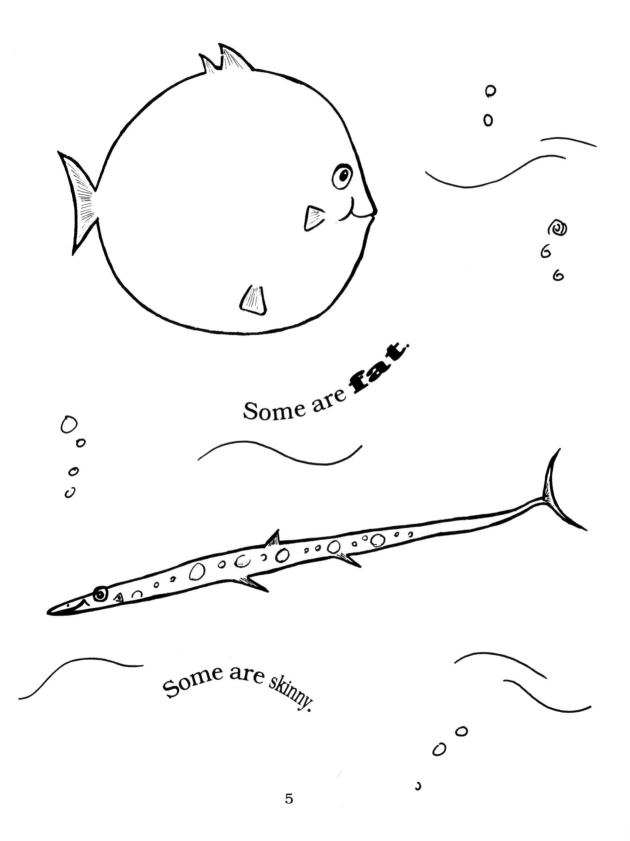

Some are **fat**.

Some are skinny.

Some are plain,

some are finny.

Some swim high,

some swim low.

Some swim fast.

Some swim slooow.

What if they all looked the same?

What if they all had the same name?

8

What if they all played the same game?

Wouldn't that be a shame?

Fish in the ocean, swimming in the water.

Each is special. That's the way it ought to be.

There's a Monster in My Closet

There's a monster in my closet.
I know because I found him.
I was looking for my sweater.
He had wrapped it all around him.

It was Sunday or Monday,
Or maybe it was Runday.
One thing was sure,
I know it was a fun day.

I had ice cream for dessert
And was feeling kind of freezing.
Mom said go outside but dress warm,
I don't want to hear you sneezing.

So I went to get my sweater,
But the monster had it on!
He was lumpy, creepy, big, and huge.
He must have weighed a ton.

I looked at him.
He looked at me.

I knew what to do.

I let out a SCREEEEAM!

I scrunched my eyes
And opened my mouth.
Got ready to *really* yell.

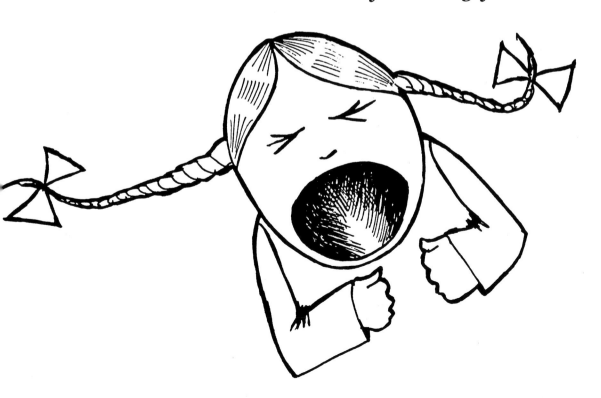

But something strange was going on.

I was sure.
I knew.
I could tell.

'Cause the monster's mouth was quivering.
His lumpy body was shivering.

He was kind of bent over
And shaking his ears.
From each of his eyes,
Fell really big tears.

I looked at him.
He looked at me.
I figured it out.
He was scared of my shout.

I said, hey,
Wait a minute.
You're a monster,
You're lumpy.

When I see you in there,
I'm supposed to get jumpy

And cover my ears
And get shaky inside.

Then run really fast
For a safe place to hide.

21

So what's the idea
Of your sniffing and crying?
You're not doing your job.
Why, you're not even trying!

If you don't quit your sobbing,
If you simply don't stop,
I'm taking you back
To the monster shop

23

And trading you in
For a monster who'll try,
Who'll holler and hiss
And be a scary guy.

Get hold of yourself!
Stand up very straight.
You'd better shape up
Before it's too late.

I looked at him.
He looked back with 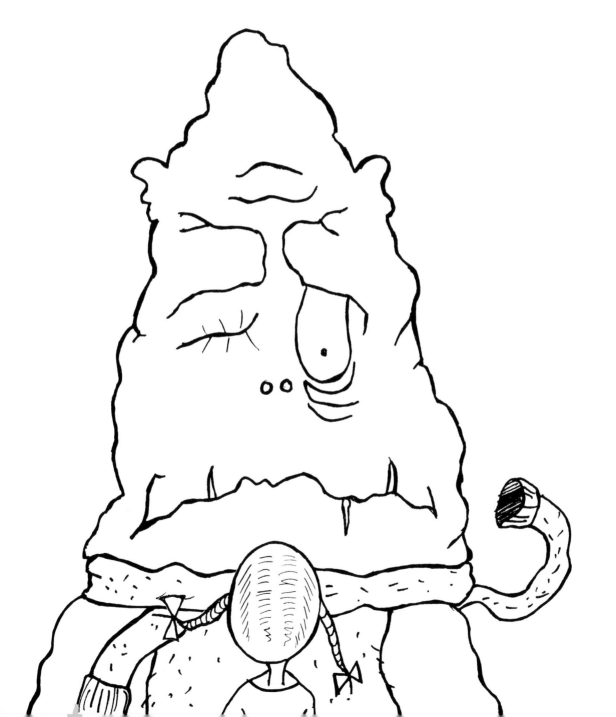ONE eye.

He shivered and quivered
And said, please can I try
To explain why I'm scared,
To explain why I cried?

I said, please make it fast
'Cause I don't have all day.
I want to go outside.
I want to go play.

He said, sure, I'll be quick,
But first could you please
Get me out of this sweater?
I am feeling quite squeezed.

So I tugged and I pulled
And I yanked and I heaved
And I huffed and I puffed
And I did get him free.

He said, whew, thanks a lot.
Thanks a trillion and three.
You're really a pal.
That was too small for me.

The reason I liked it
Was 'cause it looked snuggly.
I tried on your jacket,
But on me it looked ugly.

I waited and waited all day just to see you
Back here with the clothes and the hangers.
I thought you'd be scared,
    but instead you were mad.
What a terrible, terrible anger!

Your eyes got all tough
And your face got all rough.
Then you opened your mouth
And let out that shout.

That was something I could have
Done quite well without.

It's the first time I've heard
A sound quite so frightening.

You're a zillion times louder
Than thunder and lightning!

So I started to shake,
And I started to quake.

And my poor monster belly
Felt like strawberry jelly.

No one told me this job
Was going to be scary.

Not to mention this closet,
So dark and so chilly.

Well, that's the whole story.
Please don't think that I'm silly.

He looked at me.
I looked at him.

We stood there for almost a minute.

I said, okay, big guy,
You get one more try,
And this is the time to begin it.

He said, great, just you wait.
Then he started to stare.
If I wouldn't have known him,
I might have been scared.

Then he jumped up and down
And gave a big frown

And he showed me his teeth.
They were yucky and brown.

His paws all had claws
And his body was hairy.
But to tell you the truth,
He wasn't that scary.

He hissed and he shrieked,
Made the closet door creak.
He grunted and growled
And made slobbery sounds.

I just waited while he did
What he had to do.
Till finally he let out
A pretty good *boo*!

40

Then he stopped
And he smiled
And said, how did I do?

And he kept right on smiling
Looking prouder and prouder.

I said, not bad at all,
Though that *boo* could be louder.

But don't worry, we'll practice
Till you do it better.
Now, wait here while I get you
Daddy's old sweater.

I'm Me

I look in the mirror.
I'm **me.**

46

I sleep.
I'm **me.**

I look at something small.
I'm **me**.

I'm the smallest of all.
I'm **me**.

I paint my face.
I'm **me.**

My shadow gets big.
I'm me.

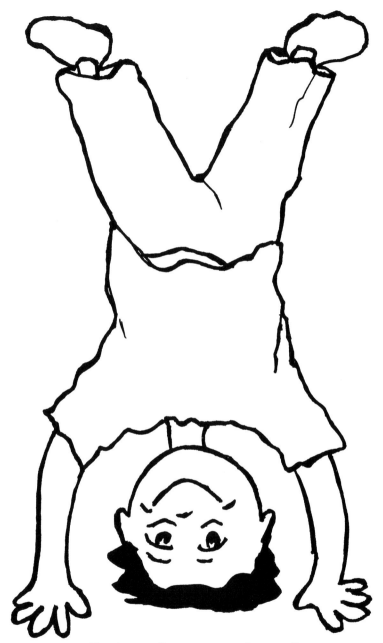

I stand on my head.
I'm **me**.

I'm me.

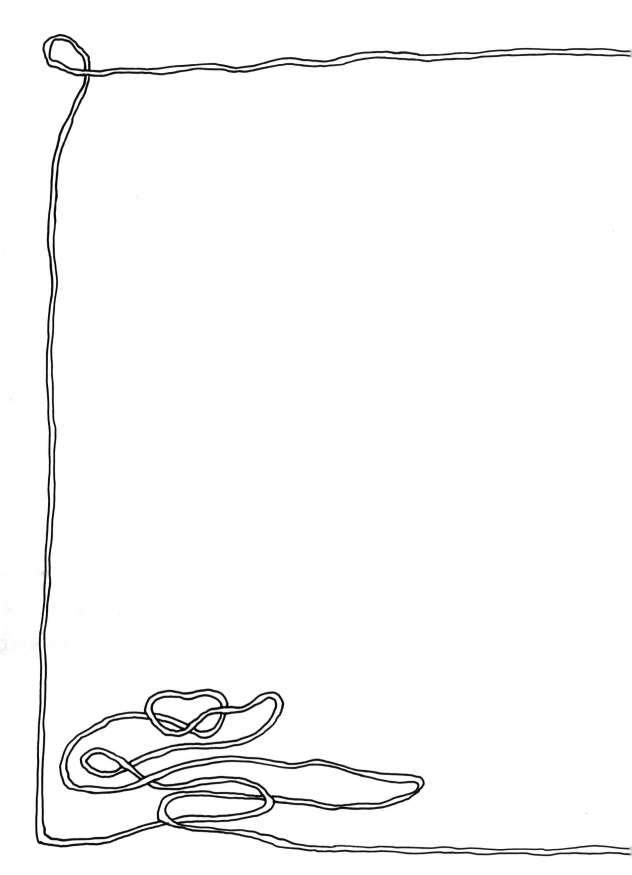

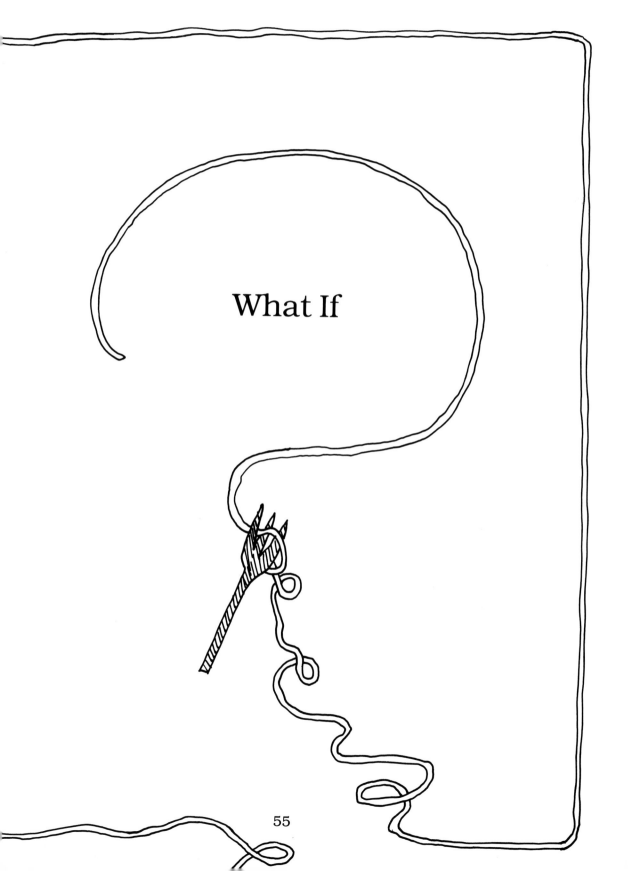

What If

What if you could call
your grandma with a banana?

What if you were
bigger than your mother?

What if dogs wore glasses?

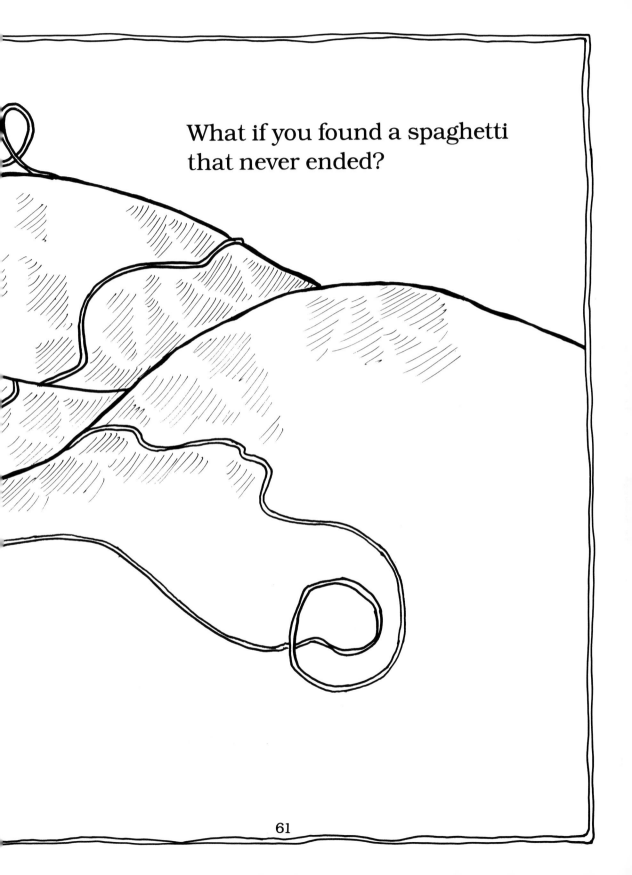

What if you found a spaghetti
that never ended?

What if *you* thought up some *what-ifs*?

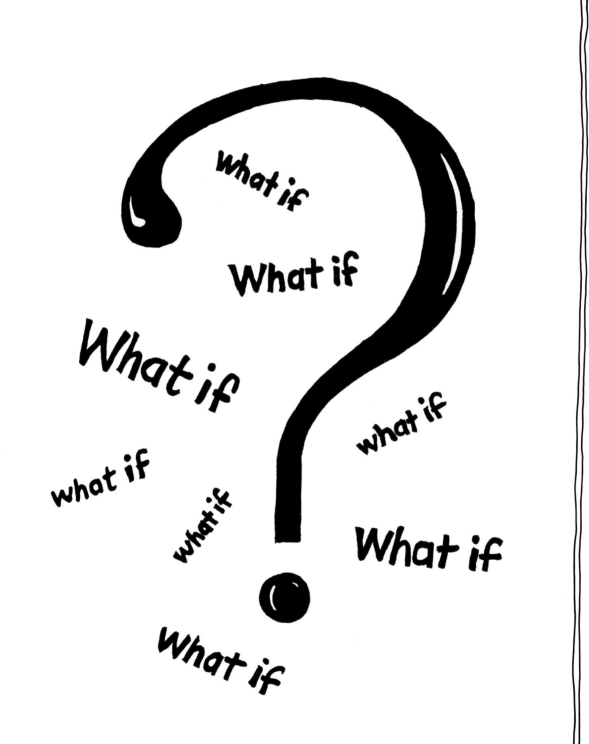

How to Get Rid of a Ghost
by Jesse Kellerman

So you want to get rid of a ghost, a ghost?
Then listen to me
I've done it the most.

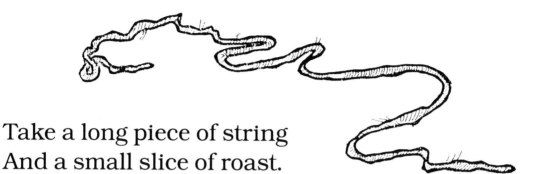

Take a long piece of string
And a small slice of roast.

This is how you get rid of a ghost, a ghost.

Take a bunch of old onions,
And two pieces of toast
And soon you won't have
    that silly old ghost.

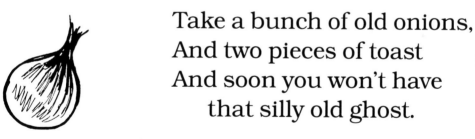

Now make a big sandwich
With the toast and the roast.
We're just about ready
To get rid of the ghost.

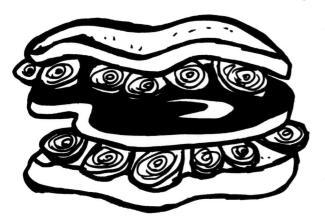

Put the **onions** in the sandwich
(That's the favorite of most)

And now we can get that silly old ghost.

Put the sandwich on the floor
And hide behind a post

And then you just wait
For a hungry old ghost.

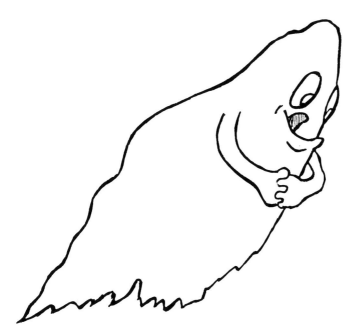

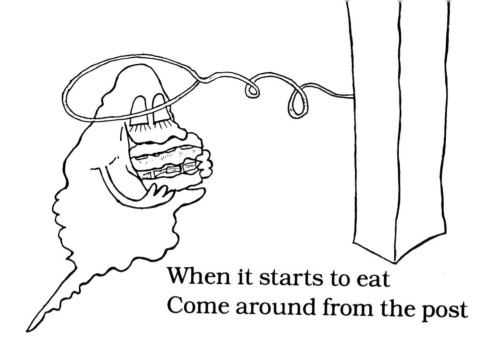

When it starts to eat
Come around from the post

And then with the string,
You tie up the ghost.

Give it some water
And be a good host

And then send away
That silly old ghost.

After you've finished
That's when you can boast.

You can tell all your friends
That you've captured a ghost.

And that is the way
To capture a ghost.

I know I am right,
I've done it the most.

Daddy, Daddy,
Can You Touch the Sky?

Daddy, Daddy,
Can you touch the sky?

Touch the sky?

I guess I can try.

I tried and tried,
But the sky's too high.

Daddy, Daddy,
Can you drink up the sea?

Drink up the sea?
Does it taste like tea?

I can't drink up the sea.
It's too big for me.

Daddy, Daddy,
Can you ride on a cloud?

Ride on a cloud?
If it makes you proud.

A cloud is just fluff

So riding it's tough.

Daddy, Daddy,
Can you stand on your nose?

Stand on my nose?
But that's for my toes.

I tried and I fell.

Think I'll use my nose to smell.

Daddy, Daddy,
But what can you do?

Hmm . . . what can I do?

Lots of things
And it's true!

I can horsey-back-ride you

And bounce you up and down.

And make funny faces

And such silly sounds.

I can throw balls
And catch them,

Pour milk in a cup,

And pour you some more
When you've drunk it all up.

I can bandage your hurt,

Wipe your tears when you're sad.

And no matter what you do
I'll never think you're bad.

I can hug you and kiss you

And tell you you're great

And tuck you in bed
When the hour grows late.

And be there to listen
When you tell me your dreams.

Or anything else,
So I guess what I mean . . .

Is

I can love you

For always
And always
And always.

ABOUT THE AUTHOR

During his fifteen-year practice as a child psychologist, Jonathan Kellerman, Ph.D., founded and directed the Psychosocial Program at Children's Hospital of Los Angeles and headed a private practice. He is a Clinical Associate Professor of Pediatrics at University of Southern California School of Medicine. He has published several dozen articles in child clinical psychology and two psychology books, including *Helping the Fearful Child*.

Now a full-time writer, Jonathan Kellerman is the author of nine consecutive bestselling novels—*The Butcher's Theater* and eight suspense novels featuring child psychologist–detective Alex Delaware: *When the Bough Breaks, Blood Test, Over the Edge, Silent Partner, Time Bomb, Private Eyes, Devil's Waltz,* and *Bad Love*. He lives in California with his wife, novelist Faye Kellerman, and their four children. His son, Jesse, contributed the poem "How to Get Rid of a Ghost" in *Daddy, Daddy, Can You Touch the Sky?*